~A BINGO BOOK~

South Dakota Bingo Book

COMPLETE BINGO GAME IN A BOOK

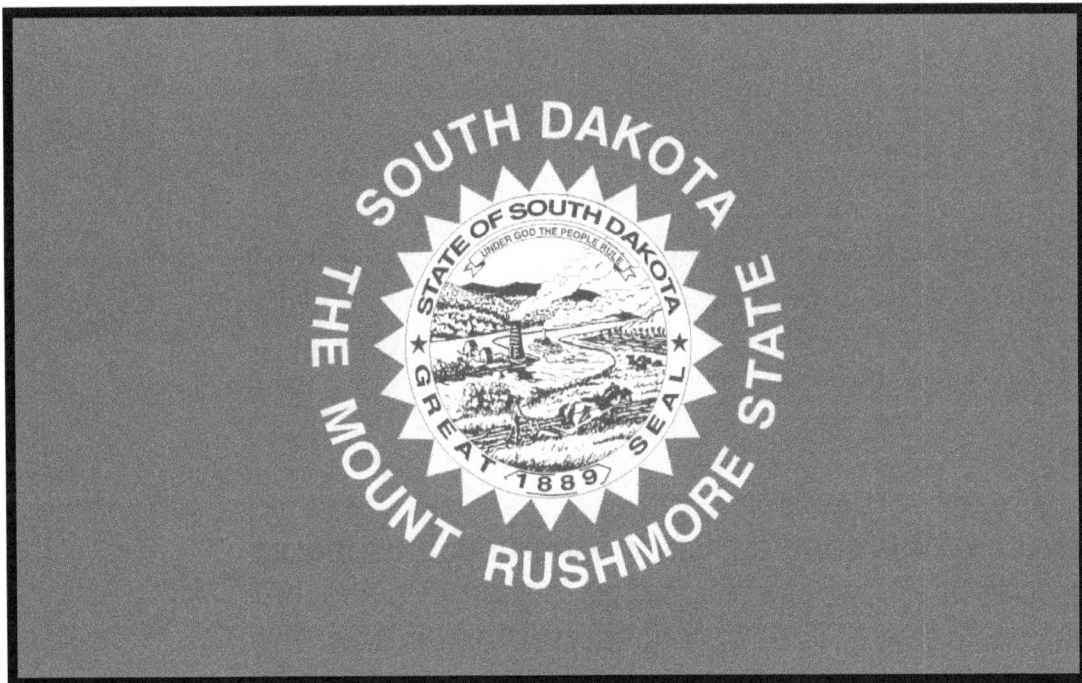

Written By Rebecca Stark

ISBN 978-0-87386-534-0

Educational Books 'n' Bingo

Printed in the U.S.A.

DIRECTIONS

INCLUDED:

List of Terms

Templates for Additional Terms and Clues

2 Clues per Term

30 Unique Bingo Cards

Markers

1. **Either cut apart the book or make copies of ALL the sheets. You might want to make an extra copy of the clue sheets to use for introduction and review. Keep the sheets in an envelope for easy reuse.**

2. Cut apart the call cards with terms and clues.

3. Pass out one bingo card per student. There are enough for a class of 30.

4. Pass out markers. You may cut apart the markers included in this book or use any other small items of your choice.

5. Decide whether or not you will require the entire card to be filled. Requiring the entire card to be filled provides a better review. However, if you have a short time to fill, you may prefer to have them do the just the border or some other format. Tell the class before you begin what is required.

6. There are 50 terms. Read the list before you begin. If there are any terms that have not been covered in class, you may want to read to the students the term and clues before you begin.

7. There is a blank space in the middle of each card. You can instruct the students to use it as a free space or you can write in answers to cover terms not included. Of course, in this case you would create your own clues. (Templates provided.)

8. Shuffle the cards and place them in a pile. Two or three clues are provided for each term. If you plan to play the game with the same group more than once, you might want to choose a different clue for each game. If not, you may choose to use more than one clue.

9. Be sure to keep the cards you have used for the present game in a separate pile. When a student calls, "Bingo," he or she will have to verify that the correct answers are on his or her card AND that the markers were placed in response to the proper questions. Pull out the cards that are on the student's card keeping them in the order they were used in the game. Read each clue as it was given and ask the student to identify the correct answer from his or her card.

10. If the student has the correct answers on the card AND has shown that they were marked in response to the *correct questions,* then that student is the winner and the game is over. If the student does not have the correct answers on the card OR he or she marked the answers in response to *the wrong questions,* then the game continues until there is a proper winner.

11. If you want to play again, reshuffle the cards and begin again.

Have fun!

TERMS INCLUDED

Agricultural	Kuchen
Badlands	Lake(s)
Black Hills	Legislature
Border(s)	Lewis and Clark
Cave	Louisiana Territory
Climate	Mined
County (-ies)	Missouri River
Coyote(s)	Motto
Crazy Horse	Mount Rushmore
Dakota Territory	Pierre
Dissected Till Plains	Prairie Coteau
Drift Prairie	Rapid City
Executive Branch	Ring-necked Pheasant
Flag	River(s)
Fry Bread	Rodeo
Fur Trade	Seal
Gold	Sioux
Great Plains	Sioux Falls
"Hail, South Dakota"	Spruce
Hall of Fame	Stone
Harney Peak	Tourism
Homesteading (-ers)	Triceratops
Honeybee(s)	Union
Jewelry	Walleye Pike
Judicial Branch	Western Wheatgrass

Additional Terms

Choose as many additional terms as you would like and write them in the squares. Repeat each as desired.
Cut out the squares and randomly distribute them to the class.
Instruct the students to place their square on the center space of their card.

Clues for
Additional Terms

Write three clues for each of your additional terms.

_____ 1. _____ 2. _____ 3. _____	_____ 1. _____ 2. _____ 3. _____
_____ 1. _____ 2. _____ 3. _____	_____ 1. _____ 2. _____ 3. _____
_____ 1. _____ 2. _____ 3. _____	_____ 1. _____ 2. _____ 3. _____

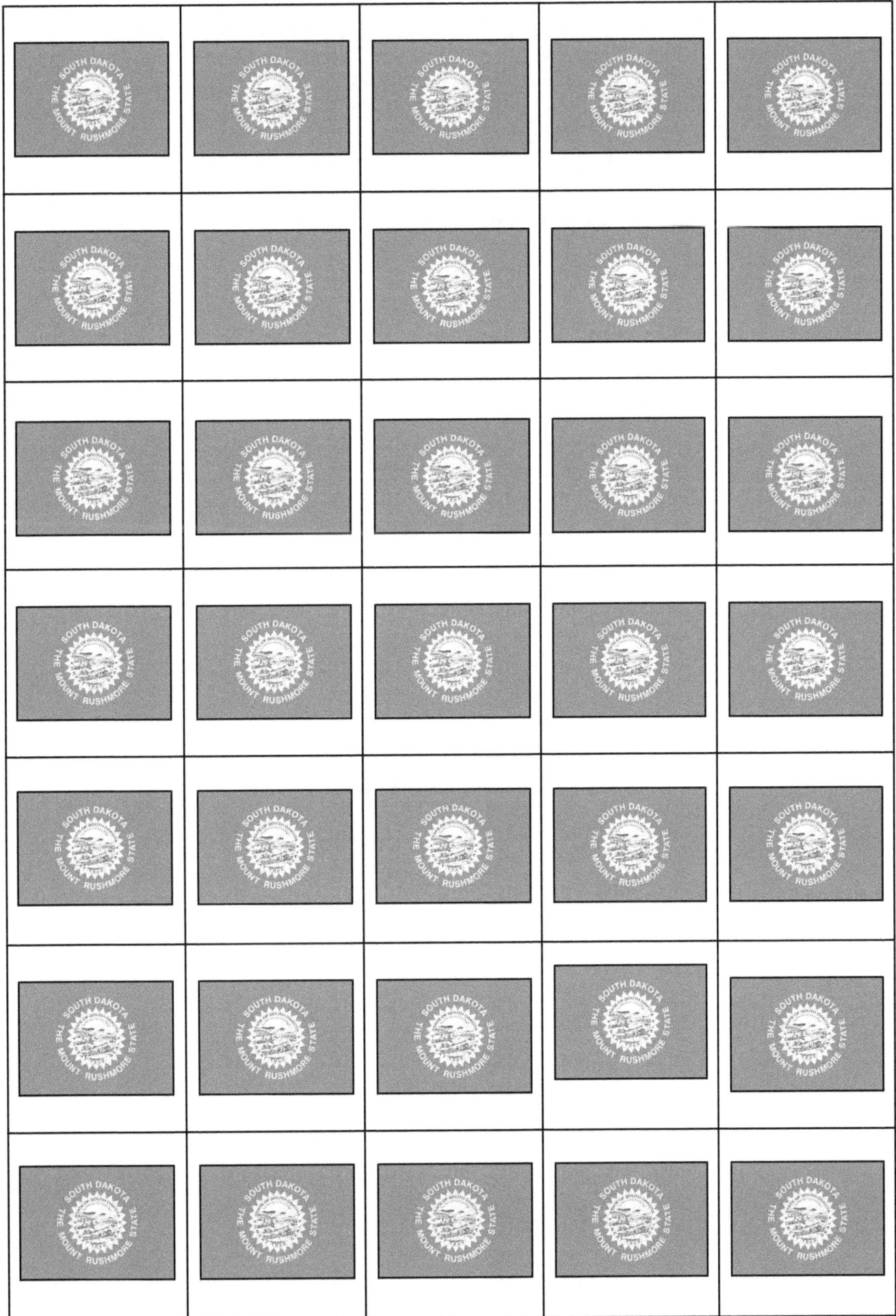

Agricultural
1. Livestock and livestock products are the state's most important ___ products.
2. Beef cattle and calves comprise more than a third of the state's total ___ receipts. Other important products are corn for grain, soybeans, sunflowers, rye, wheat, and hogs.

Badlands
1. ___ were created long ago by the erosion of extremely soft sedimentary rocks by wind and water.
2. ___ National Park is east of the Black Hills in the Great Plains region.

Black Hills
1. The ___ are in the southwestern part of the state. These rough, heavily forested mountains extend into Wyoming.
2. Jewel Cave, Wind Cave, and Mount Rushmore are all in the ___. So is Harney Peak, the highest point in the state.

Border(s)
1. North Dakota, Nebraska, Minnesota, Iowa, Montana, and Wyoming ___ South Dakota.
2. The Standing Rock Indian Reservation is a Lakota, Yanktonai and Dakota Indian reservation. It is on the ___ of North and South Dakota.

Cave
1. Wind ___, which is near Hot Springs, and Jewel ___, which is near Custer, are both within the Black Hills.
2. Jewel ___ is the second longest ___ in the world. It has more than 160 miles of mapped passages.

Climate
1. South Dakota has an interior continental ___, with hot summers, very cold winters, high winds, and occasional droughts.
2. South Dakota has a temperate continental ___, with four distinct seasons. Precipitation ranges from moderate in the east to semi-arid in the west.

County (-ies)
1. There are 66 ___ in South Dakota.
2. Minnehaha ___ has the largest population.

Coyote(s)
1. The ___ is the state animal.
2. ___ are also called prairie wolves. Many are in the Black Hills and along the Missouri River and its tributaries.

Crazy Horse
1. Sitting Bull and ___ were Sioux leaders. ___ led a war party to victory at the Battle of the Little Bighorn.
2. The ___ Memorial is a mountain monument under construction in the Black Hills.

Dakota Territory
1. When it was created in 1861, ___ included much of present-day Montana and Wyoming as well as North and South Dakota.
2. In 1883 the capital of ___ moved from Yankton to Bismarck.

Dissected Till Plains 1. The ___ extend into the southeastern corner of the state from Iowa and Nebraska. This fertile region is characterized by rolling hills. 2. Like the Drift Prairie, the ___ were carved out hundreds of thousands of years ago by the movement of glaciers.	**Drift Prairie** 1. The ___, also known as the Prairie Hills, covers most of eastern South Dakota. It is characterized by low hills and glacial lakes. 2. The ___ is a rolling plain covered with glacial drift. Sioux Falls is in this region on the banks of the Big Sioux River.
Executive Branch 1. The ___ of state government comprises the governor, lt. governor, attorney general, secretary of state, treasurer, and various commissions and departments. 2. The governor is head of the ___ of state government. The present-day governor is [fill in].	**Flag** 1. The state ___ features the state seal on a blazing sun centered on a sky blue field. 2. The name of the state is above the seal on the state ___. Below the seal is the state nickname, Mount Rushmore State.
Fry Bread 1. Also known as "squaw bread" in some areas, ___ is a Native American food. 2. ___ is an official state symbol. It is made by frying the flat dough in oil, shortening, or lard.	**Fur Trade** 1. ___ was established in the area by the time of Lewis and Clark, but it increased after they described the abundance of buffalo, beaver, and river otter. 2. The French controlled the ___ in the New World until 1610 when Henry Hudson discovered Hudson's Bay while sailing for England.
Gold 1. The discovery of ___ in 1874 caused a rush of miners, prospectors, and fortune seekers to the Black Hills. 2. The discovery of___ brought many miners into the Black Hills, an area that was sacred to the Indians. This led to the Sioux War of 1876.	**Great Plains** 1. The ___ region covers most of the western two-thirds of the state. This region is separated from the Drift Prairie by the James River Basin. 2. The Missouri Coteau, or the Missouri Hills, are in the ___ region. So are the Badlands.
"Hail, South Dakota" 1. ___ is the state song. 2. This march was written by Deecourt Hammitt. It became the official state song in 1943.	**Hall of Fame** 1. The South Dakota ___ is in Chamberlain. 2. Tom Brokaw, Sitting Bull, and Crazy Horse are among the inductees to the South Dakota ___.

South Dakota Bingo

Harney Peak 1. At 7,242 feet, ___ is the highest point in the state. 2. ___ is located within the Black Elk Wilderness area. It is in the Black Hills National Forest.	**Homesteading (-ers)** 1. Dakota Territory opened for ___ in 1863. After living on and improving 160 acres of land for a number of years, people could get the land for free. 2. ___ could receive an additional 160 acres by planting and maintaining trees on the prairie.
Honeybee(s) 1. The ___ is the state insect. 2. The ___ is an official state symbol in seventeen states, probably because it plays such an important role in agriculture.	**Jewelry** 1. Black Hills gold is the official ___. 2. Only ___ manufactured in the Black Hills can be called Black Hills gold.
Judicial Branch 1. The ___ of the state government interprets the laws. 2. The ___ of the state government includes a Supreme Court and trial courts called Circuit Courts. The Supreme Court is the highest court.	**Kuchen** 1. ___ is the German word for "cake." It is the official state dessert. 2. ___ desserts are popular in areas of German settlement, including South Dakota.
Lake(s) 1. Oahe, Francis Case, Lewis and Clark, and Waubay are ___ in South Dakota. 2. ___ Oahe begins in central South Dakota and continues into North Dakota. By volume, it is the fourth-largest reservoir in the United States.	**Legislature** 1. The South Dakota ___ comprises the South Dakota Senate and the South Dakota House of Representatives. 2. The South Dakota ___ makes the laws.
Lewis and Clark 1. The ___ Expedition explored present-day South Dakota's stretch of the Missouri River in 1804. 2. Explorers ___ visited present-day South Dakota in 1804 and again in 1806. The state highways 1804 and 1806 commemorate their expedition. South Dakota Bingo	**Louisiana Territory** 1. Much of present-day South Dakota was part of the ___, which the United States purchased from France in 1803; the rest was acquired in the Treaty of 1818. 2. ___ was renamed Missouri Territory to avoid confusion when Louisiana joined the Union in 1812. © Barbara M. Peller

Mined
1. Granite, clays, limestone, crushed stone, sand and gravel, and petroleum are South Dakota's most important ___ products.
2. Gold was an important ___ product until the Homestake Mine was closed in 2001.

Missouri River
1. The capital city of Pierre is located on the ___. It is the longest river in the nation.
2. The ___ runs through the central part of South Dakota, dividing the state into what is often called East River and West River.

Motto
1. "Under God, the People Rule" is the state ___.
2. The South Dakota ___ appears on the great seal.

Mount Rushmore
1. This mountain sculpture of 4 Presidents was created by Gutzon Borglum over a period of 14 years.
2. ___ features the faces of George Washington, Thomas Jefferson, Theodore Roosevelt, and Abraham Lincoln.

Pierre
1. ___, the capital of South Dakota, is in the Great Plains region.
2. ___ is the second least populous state capital after Montpelier, Vermont.

Prairie Coteau (Coteau des Prairies)
1. The ___ is a plateau about 200 miles in length and 100 miles in width. It rises from the prairie flatlands in eastern South Dakota.
2. This plateau is composed of thick glacial deposits. The region has many small glacial lakes and is drained by the Big Sioux River.

Rapid City
1. ___ is the second largest city in the state. It is known as the "Gateway to the Black Hills."
2. ___ is sometimes called "The City of Presidents." Its downtown district features a series of life-size bronze statues of past presidents.

Ring-necked Pheasant
1. The Chinese ___ is the state bird.
2. This bird is shown flying over Mount Rushmore on the state quarter.

River(s)
1. The Missouri, Cheyenne, James, and White are ___ in South Dakota.
2. The Missouri is the longest ___ in the nation. With its tributaries, it drains almost the entire state.

Rodeo
1. ___ is the official state sport.
2. The first ___ in South Dakota is thought to have taken place in Rosebud in the late 1890s. The sport developed as cowboys began competing against one another.

South Dakota Bingo

Seal 1. The mining industry is represented on the left bank of the river on the Great ___. Agriculture is represented on the east bank. 2. The steamboat on the Great ___ represents trade and transportation.	**Sioux** 1. There are 8 federally recognized ___ tribes in South Dakota.* 2. Sitting Bull and Crazy Horse were ___ leaders. *The federally recognized tribes are Cheyenne River, Crow Creek, Flandreau Santee, Lower Brule, Oglala, Rosebud, the Sisseton-Wahpeton and the Yankton.
Sioux Falls 1. ___ is the largest city in the state. 2. ___ is situated in Great Plains on the banks of the Big Sioux River.	**Spruce** 1. The Black Hills ___ is the state tree. 2. The Black Hills ___ has a dense, bright, bluish-green foliage.
Stone 1. Fairburn agate is the state gem___. 2. Rose quartz is the state mineral ___.	**Triceratops** 1. ___ is the official state fossil. 2. ___ fossil specimens have been found in Harding, Perkins, Corson, Dewey, Ziebach, Meade, and Butte counties.
Tourism 1. Agriculture, mining, and ___ are important industries. 2. ___ is an important industry. Mount Rushmore is visited by almost three million people each year.	**Union** 1. North and South Dakota were admitted to the ___ on November 2, 1889. 2. No one knows which of the Dakotas was admitted to the ___ first. Because North Dakota comes first alphabetically, it is said to be the 39th state and South Dakota is said to be the 40th.
Walleye Pike 1. The ___ is the state fish. 2. ___ are found throughout the state. They require a cool-water habitat and occur mostly in the eastern glacial lakes and in the Missouri River reservoirs. South Dakota Bingo	**Western Wheatgrass** 1. ___ is the state grass. 2. This tough native grass can be found throughout the entire state. © Barbara M. Peller

South Dakota Bingo

Rapid City	Agricultural	Black Hills	"Hail, South Dakota"	Cave
Gold	Badlands	Union	Lewis and Clark	Rodeo
Triceratops	Legislature		Mount Rushmore	Walleye Pike
Stone	River(s)	Spruce	Lake(s)	Mined
Motto	Homesteading (-ers)	Flag	Sioux	Jewelry

South Dakota Bingo

Stone	Triceratops	Tourism	Ring-necked Pheasant	Kuchen
Mined	Fry Bread	Coyote(s)	River(s)	Missouri River
Dakota Territory	Homesteading (-ers)		Honeybee(s)	Spruce
Pierre	Prairie Coteau	Legislature	Western Wheatgrass	Cave
Rodeo	Union	Flag	Gold	Sioux

South Dakota Bingo: Card No. 2

South Dakota Bingo

Homesteading (-ers)	Spruce	Fry Bread	Lake(s)	Triceratops
Mined	Badlands	Crazy Horse	Agricultural	Harney Peak
River(s)	Union		Missouri River	Border(s)
Legislature	Dakota Territory	Motto	Pierre	Tourism
Sioux	Dissected Till Plains	Flag	Western Wheatgrass	Kuchen

South Dakota Bingo: Card No. 3

South Dakota Bingo

Legislature	Missouri River	Black Hills	Dissected Till Plains	Kuchen
Louisiana Territory	County (-ies)	Agricultural	Ring-necked Pheasant	Triceratops
Mount Rushmore	Pierre		Jewelry	"Hail, South Dakota"
Spruce	Badlands	Union	Flag	Coyote(s)
Drift Prairie	Rodeo	Climate	Sioux	Walleye Pike

South Dakota Bingo

Rodeo	Cave	River(s)	Coyote(s)	Dissected Till Plains
Louisiana Territory	Spruce	Crazy Horse	Honeybee(s)	Badlands
Black Hills	Walleye Pike		Lewis and Clark	Hall of Fame
Jewelry	Kuchen	Rapid City	Western Wheatgrass	Executive Branch
Fry Bread	Flag	Triceratops	Legislature	Mount Rushmore

© Barbara M. Peller

South Dakota Bingo

Border(s)	Missouri River	Tourism	Kuchen	Walleye Pike
Lake(s)	River(s)	Executive Branch	Agricultural	Triceratops
Ring-necked Pheasant	Drift Prairie		County (-ies)	Honeybee(s)
Flag	Motto	Western Wheatgrass	Climate	Black Hills
Mined	Coyote(s)	Rapid City	Mount Rushmore	Fur Trade

South Dakota Bingo: Card No. 6

South Dakota Bingo

Rapid City	Missouri River	Hall of Fame	Spruce	Fry Bread
Mined	Kuchen	Homesteading (-ers)	Badlands	Louisiana Territory
Walleye Pike	"Hail, South Dakota"		Honeybee(s)	County (-ies)
Legislature	Pierre	Crazy Horse	Stone	Dakota Territory
Flag	Dissected Till Plains	Western Wheatgrass	Climate	Border(s)

South Dakota Bingo: Card No. 7

South Dakota Bingo

Mount Rushmore	Missouri River	Great Plains	Lake(s)	County (-ies)
Louisiana Territory	Black Hills	Ring-necked Pheasant	Walleye Pike	Coyote(s)
Fur Trade	Dissected Till Plains		Kuchen	Cave
Sioux	Legislature	Stone	Drift Prairie	Pierre
Union	Flag	Climate	River(s)	Mined

South Dakota Bingo: Card No. 8

South Dakota Bingo

Honeybee(s)	Fry Bread	Homesteading (-ers)	Fur Trade	Dissected Till Plains
Drift Prairie	Kuchen	Mount Rushmore	River(s)	Missouri River
Harney Peak	Rapid City		Badlands	Great Plains
Executive Branch	Cave	Motto	Lewis and Clark	Hall of Fame
Pierre	Western Wheatgrass	Crazy Horse	Stone	Jewelry

South Dakota Bingo: Card No. 9

© Barbara M. Peller

South Dakota Bingo

Stone	Lake(s)	County (-ies)	Ring-necked Pheasant	Fur Trade
Walleye Pike	Coyote(s)	Agricultural	Badlands	Kuchen
Dissected Till Plains	Missouri River		"Hail, South Dakota"	Dakota Territory
Motto	Jewelry	Executive Branch	Western Wheatgrass	Harney Peak
Crazy Horse	Mined	Tourism	Rodeo	Mount Rushmore

South Dakota Bingo: Card No. 10

South Dakota Bingo

Border(s)	Missouri River	River(s)	Executive Branch	Mined
Great Plains	Harney Peak	Lewis and Clark	Honeybee(s)	Agricultural
Louisiana Territory	Kuchen		Tourism	Homesteading (-ers)
Crazy Horse	Triceratops	Western Wheatgrass	Dissected Till Plains	Stone
Drift Prairie	Flag	Rapid City	Climate	Fry Bread

South Dakota Bingo

Fry Bread	Cave	Harney Peak	Lake(s)	Honeybee(s)
Homesteading (-ers)	Mined	Black Hills	Climate	Badlands
Rapid City	Hall of Fame		Walleye Pike	Ring-necked Pheasant
Flag	Pierre	Kuchen	Stone	Louisiana Territory
Missouri River	Great Plains	Dissected Till Plains	Drift Prairie	Coyote(s)

South Dakota Bingo

Executive Branch	Cave	Border(s)	Harney Peak	Walleye Pike
Black Hills	Great Plains	Kuchen	Honeybee(s)	Dakota Territory
Lake(s)	Coyote(s)		Homesteading (-ers)	Hall of Fame
Mount Rushmore	Western Wheatgrass	County (-ies)	Dissected Till Plains	Stone
Flag	Jewelry	Climate	Rapid City	Lewis and Clark

South Dakota Bingo: Card No. 13

South Dakota Bingo

Gold	Kuchen	River(s)	Honeybee(s)	Drift Prairie
Coyote(s)	Rapid City	Harney Peak	Badlands	Missouri River
Executive Branch	"Hail, South Dakota"		Tourism	Crazy Horse
Jewelry	Western Wheatgrass	Dissected Till Plains	County (-ies)	Border(s)
Flag	Ring-necked Pheasant	Dakota Territory	Mined	Mount Rushmore

South Dakota Bingo: Card No. 14

South Dakota Bingo

Lewis and Clark	Honeybee(s)	River(s)	Fry Bread	Lake(s)
Border(s)	Tourism	Agricultural	Black Hills	Drift Prairie
Walleye Pike	Rapid City		Triceratops	Missouri River
Flag	Harney Peak	Great Plains	Western Wheatgrass	Executive Branch
Mined	Pierre	Climate	Fur Trade	Homesteading (-ers)

South Dakota Bingo: Card No. 15

South Dakota Bingo

County (-ies)	Harney Peak	Great Plains	Fur Trade	Prairie Coteau
Ring-necked Pheasant	Dakota Territory	Hall of Fame	Louisiana Territory	"Hail, South Dakota"
Executive Branch	Cave		Walleye Pike	Homesteading (-ers)
Legislature	Coyote(s)	Flag	Lewis and Clark	Stone
Drift Prairie	Sioux Falls	Climate	Pierre	Missouri River

South Dakota Bingo: Card No. 16

South Dakota Bingo

Crazy Horse	Seal	Judicial Branch	Harney Peak	Gold
Lewis and Clark	Drift Prairie	Western Wheatgrass	"Hail, South Dakota"	Hall of Fame
Honeybee(s)	Mount Rushmore		Sioux Falls	Great Plains
Jewelry	Mined	Stone	River(s)	Dakota Territory
Motto	Executive Branch	Fry Bread	Lake(s)	Cave

South Dakota Bingo: Card No. 17

South Dakota Bingo

Fur Trade	Dissected Till Plains	Coyote(s)	Executive Branch	Ring-necked Pheasant
Missouri River	Crazy Horse	Motto	Walleye Pike	Drift Prairie
Honeybee(s)	Dakota Territory		Judicial Branch	Black Hills
Cave	Agricultural	Western Wheatgrass	Stone	Tourism
Sioux Falls	Harney Peak	River(s)	Seal	Border(s)

South Dakota Bingo: Card No. 18

South Dakota Bingo

Walleye Pike	Border(s)	Harney Peak	Great Plains	Stone
Lewis and Clark	Lake(s)	Missouri River	Fry Bread	"Hail, South Dakota"
Seal	Dissected Till Plains		Badlands	Triceratops
Tourism	Sioux Falls	Motto	Pierre	Judicial Branch
Black Hills	Prairie Coteau	Mined	Mount Rushmore	Climate

South Dakota Bingo: Card No. 19

South Dakota Bingo

Gold	Seal	Lake(s)	Harney Peak	Climate
Coyote(s)	Homesteading (-ers)	Louisiana Territory	Motto	Ring-necked Pheasant
Cave	Hall of Fame		Legislature	Agricultural
Rodeo	Union	Sioux	Pierre	Sioux Falls
Spruce	Mount Rushmore	Prairie Coteau	Stone	Judicial Branch

South Dakota Bingo: Card No. 20

South Dakota Bingo

Lewis and Clark	Border(s)	Louisiana Territory	Harney Peak	Rodeo
Cave	Judicial Branch	County (-ies)	Great Plains	Rapid City
Dakota Territory	Mined		Seal	River(s)
Motto	Fry Bread	Sioux Falls	Jewelry	Mount Rushmore
Legislature	Prairie Coteau	Climate	Crazy Horse	Pierre

South Dakota Bingo

Fur Trade	Tourism	Judicial Branch	Black Hills	Executive Branch
Ring-necked Pheasant	Lake(s)	Triceratops	Great Plains	Badlands
Coyote(s)	"Hail, South Dakota"		Rapid City	Hall of Fame
Sioux Falls	Jewelry	Pierre	Agricultural	Louisiana Territory
Prairie Coteau	Crazy Horse	Seal	Dakota Territory	Legislature

South Dakota Bingo

County (-ies)	Seal	Fry Bread	Black Hills	Climate
Border(s)	Gold	Mined	Lewis and Clark	Agricultural
Tourism	Executive Branch		Sioux	Rapid City
Dakota Territory	Prairie Coteau	Sioux Falls	Crazy Horse	Pierre
Rodeo	Union	Mount Rushmore	Motto	Judicial Branch

South Dakota Bingo

County (-ies)	Mount Rushmore	Gold	Seal	Great Plains
Judicial Branch	Climate	Louisiana Territory	Ring-necked Pheasant	Rapid City
Hall of Fame	Fur Trade		Executive Branch	Dakota Territory
Rodeo	Sioux	Sioux Falls	Crazy Horse	Cave
Spruce	Legislature	Prairie Coteau	Lake(s)	Union

South Dakota Bingo

Legislature	Louisiana Territory	Seal	River(s)	Judicial Branch
Agricultural	Cave	Lewis and Clark	County (-ies)	Badlands
Jewelry	Great Plains		Sioux	Sioux Falls
Triceratops	Rodeo	Union	Prairie Coteau	"Hail, South Dakota"
Climate	Gold	Coyote(s)	Drift Prairie	Spruce

South Dakota Bingo: Card No. 25

© Barbara M. Peller

South Dakota Bingo

Judicial Branch	Seal	Tourism	Ring-necked Pheasant	Fur Trade
Motto	Lake(s)	Great Plains	Gold	County (-ies)
Jewelry	Sioux		"Hail, South Dakota"	Legislature
Crazy Horse	Black Hills	Rodeo	Prairie Coteau	Sioux Falls
Hall of Fame	Drift Prairie	River(s)	Union	Spruce

South Dakota Bingo

Tourism	Coyote(s)	Seal	Gold	Homesteading (-ers)
Rodeo	Sioux	Lewis and Clark	Sioux Falls	Badlands
Western Wheatgrass	Union		Prairie Coteau	Legislature
Fur Trade	Border(s)	Louisiana Territory	Spruce	Agricultural
Drift Prairie	"Hail, South Dakota"	Judicial Branch	Triceratops	Hall of Fame

South Dakota Bingo: Card No. 27

South Dakota Bingo

Tourism	Gold	Triceratops	Seal	County (-ies)
Homesteading (-ers)	Judicial Branch	Sioux	Ring-necked Pheasant	"Hail, South Dakota"
Union	Dakota Territory		Hall of Fame	Motto
Stone	Fur Trade	Mined	Prairie Coteau	Sioux Falls
Black Hills	Honeybee(s)	Drift Prairie	Spruce	Rodeo

South Dakota Bingo

Judicial Branch	Gold	Fur Trade	Lewis and Clark	Honeybee(s)
Pierre	Motto	Louisiana Territory	Hall of Fame	Triceratops
Jewelry	Sioux		Badlands	Seal
Homesteading (-ers)	Rodeo	Kuchen	Prairie Coteau	Sioux Falls
County (-ies)	Great Plains	Spruce	Border(s)	Union

South Dakota Bingo

Dissected Till Plains	Seal	Ring-necked Pheasant	Honeybee(s)	Sioux Falls
Agricultural	Gold	Tourism	"Hail, South Dakota"	Badlands
Jewelry	Executive Branch		Hall of Fame	Louisiana Territory
Spruce	Border(s)	Black Hills	Prairie Coteau	Sioux
Rodeo	Walleye Pike	Union	Judicial Branch	Triceratops

South Dakota Bingo: Card No. 30

www.ingramcontent.com/pod-product-compliance
Lightning Source LLC
LaVergne TN
LVHW061339060426
835511LV00014B/2002